Totally Extreme Sports

Sarah Fleming

A Quiz

See if you can answer the questions in this book about extreme sports.

Contents

Trackers

Photo Gallery

Rock climbing

Skateboarding

White-water rafting

Extreme scuba diving

Extreme sports can be dangerous! Sometimes extreme sports are an extreme form of a well-known sport, sometimes they are new sports. Use the pictures on these pages to help you answer some of the questions in this book.

Ice climbing

Snowboarding

Boogie boarding

Mogul skiing

Can you think of any other extreme sports?

Introduction

Skiing down a gentle slope is not an extreme sport. Doing 360° turns off a ski jump is.

Extreme kayaking

Extreme skiing

Some extreme sports can look weird.

Extreme sport:
1. a dangerous sport
2. a form of a sport that takes that sport to its limits

Extreme unicycling

Yet they are all dangerous.

If you want to take up an extreme sport, you need the right training by professional people.

Gear

Harness

Boots

Ice axe

Deadman

Shovel

Ice screw

Carabiners

Sunglasses

Crampons

Helmet

Warm clothing

Jumar

You need the right gear for extreme sports. Having the right gear means you can do the sport correctly, and it makes you less likely to hurt yourself.

Which sport do you need this gear for?

Look at the pieces of gear outlined in red. **What do you think they are used for?**

Look back at pages 2–3 to help you.

This gear is for **ice climbing**.

You can stab an ice axe into ice or snow to help you climb.

You use it to break up ice.

Ice climbing: to climb ice- and snow-covered mountains

Sunglasses protect your eyes from the strong glare of the sun off the ice and snow.

They also protect your eyes from falling ice and snow.

A harness hooks on to the rope and your body. It must be strong, to hold you if you fall.

Crampons dig into ice to help you climb up a steep slope.

They keep you from sliding or falling down.

A deadman digs into ice. You can attach your rope to it and it holds you if you fall.

Do the Boogie!

Look at these pictures of boogie boarders riding the waves. One shows the right way to boogie board. One shows how *not* to boogie board. Which is which?

If you wipe out – fall in – remember to hold your breath! You should be tied to your board by a cord, so you won't lose it.

Standing up on a boogie board takes a lot of practice. Back flips are hard.

Boogie boarding is easier than **surfing** because the boards are lighter and shorter. You can do most surfing tricks with a boogie board. Boogie boards are also cheaper!

Boogie boarding: to ride the waves as surfers do. To get up high on top of a wave and do tricks.

Surfing: to "ride" a wave for as long as possible and do tricks as you go

Compare and Contrast

Look at this list. It tells you eight things about paragliding.

For paragliding you need:
1. a parachute
2. a helmet
3. a harness
4. a high place to start
5. to jump off a high place
6. to control where you go
7. air currents to lift you up
8. no help to get into the air.

Paragliding

Look at these two photos of extreme sports. Which things are the same, and which are different?

Parasailing

Paragliding: to fly with a parachute by jumping off a high place and catching warm winds

Parasailing: to fly with a parachute by being towed by a boat or car. Sometimes parasailors can free themselves from the tow once they are high in the air.

Different	The Same
For parasailing you: <ul><li>don't need a high place to start</li><li>start by being towed up by a boat or a car</li><li>can't control where you go – the boat or car controls this</li><li>don't need air currents to lift you up</li><li>need other people to drive the boat/car.</li></ul>	For parasailing and paragliding you: <ul><li>use a parachute</li><li>wear a helmet</li><li>wear a harness.</li></ul>

Look at this sport. What is different between this sport and paragliding?

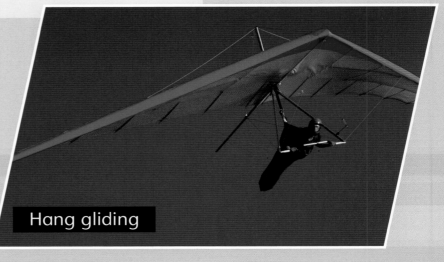

Hang gliding

Oops!

Extreme sports can cause injuries. Different extreme sports are bad for different parts of the body. Sometimes this is because of the way you fall, or because of the pressure the sport puts on different areas of your body.

Look at these three injuries.

Look at these three sports.

Snowboarding:
to go down a hill on a single board rather than on two, such as for skiing

A

B

Mogul skiing:
in this kind of skiing, you go down a steep, bumpy run as quickly as you can

Bungee jumping:
to jump from a height of 260–400 feet (79–122m), attached to an elastic cord – and live!

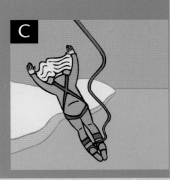
C

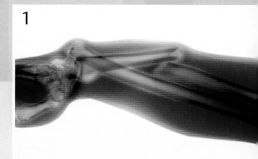
1

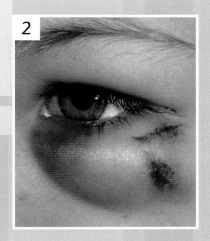
2

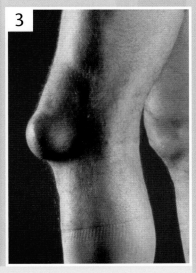
3

Which sport do you think caused which injury?

A = 1

The most common snowboarding injury is to the arm. This happens when you put out your arm to stop a fall. This can break your arm.

B = 3

Mogul skiing is bumpy. Your knees move a lot and get bumped. Knees often get injured.

C = 2

Your eyes can be damaged by the changes in the forces you feel as you bounce up and down when you do a bungee jump. Sometimes your eyes can be damaged forever.

Which Water?

1

2

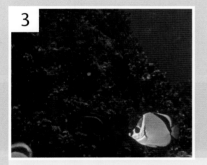

3

4

Which water goes with which sport?

C

White -water rafting: to get your raft safely down rapids on a river

B

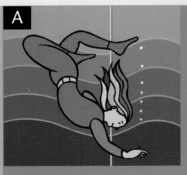

A

Free diving: to dive deep and as long as possible without breathing apparatus

Bog snorkeling: to "swim" through the mucky water of a bog, keeping your head underwater, wearing fins, and not using any normal swimming stroke

D

Scuba diving: to dive underwater with the help of tanks that give you air to breathe

1 = C

You need white-water rapids to do white-water rafting.

3 = D

You can scuba dive in many places, but it's nice to see sea life while you're diving.

2 = B

A bog is an area of wet, spongy ground. Bog snorkelers cut ditches into bogs. The ditches fill with earthy, brown water.

4 = A

Free divers like to dive straight down, deep into the sea.

The record for a free dive is 558 feet (170 m).

Headgear

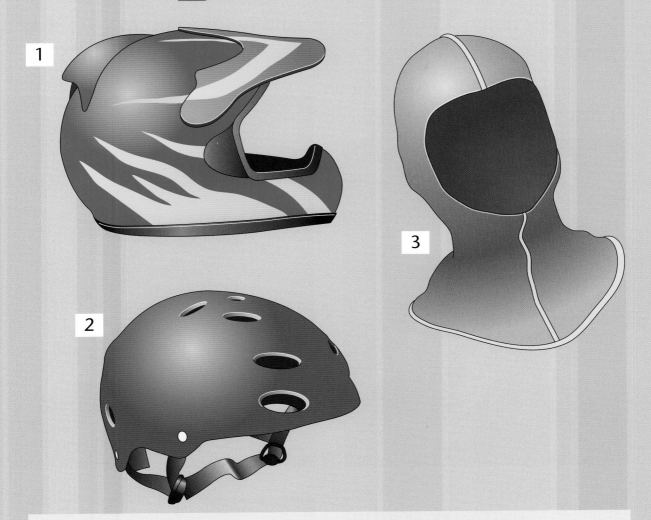

Look at the pictures of different kinds of headgear.
They are for different extreme sports.
Which headgear goes with which one of these sports?

A Motocross
B Extreme scuba diving
C Aggressive skating

A = 1 Motocross

Motocross is a fast sport that uses heavy, hard machines. This headgear is a helmet and is worn to protect you if you crash.

B = 3 Extreme scuba diving

This headgear is made of metal and helps to protect you when you go diving with sharks.

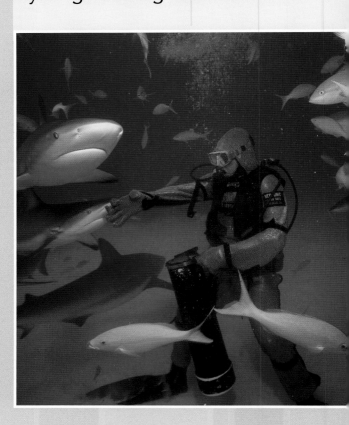

C = 2 Aggressive skating

Aggressive skaters use helmets that are a little like bicycle helmets. They keep you safe, and their shape helps you go fast. The world speed record for aggressive skating is 62 mph (100 kph).

What Is It?

You can do it…
in the desert…
on ice…
on mountaintops…
in a half-pipe.

Which extreme sport is it?

Extreme Cycling

You can take a bike almost anywhere.
This can be dangerous – wear the right gear!

Bungee

Look at this picture of a bungee jumper. Imagine you want to set up a bungee-jumping business.

Can you list the gear you would need for a bungee-jumping business? Can you explain what each piece of gear is for?

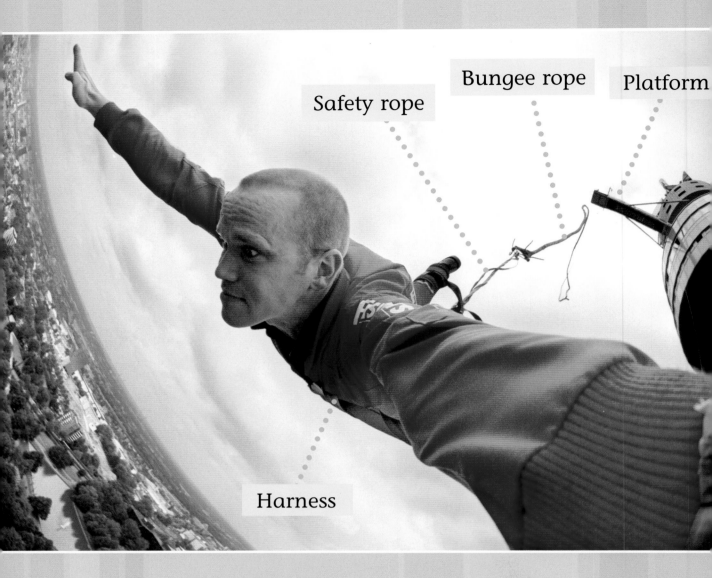

Safety rope

Bungee rope

Platform

Harness

Bungee rope:
elastic, nylon, and rubber rope. This keeps you from falling to the ground when you jump.

Harness:
attaches you to the rope

Platform:
where you jump from

Safety rope:
same as a bungee rope – a second rope in case the first one breaks

Lingo

Read these phrases and look at the pictures.
Guess which extreme sport the phrases come from.
Guess what they mean!

A Zooed out **C** Free fall
B Goofy   **D** Pitch

A = 1

Zooed out:
boogie boarding – crowded surf

B = 3

Goofy:
snowboarding – riding with your right foot forward

C = 4

Free fall:
bungee jumping – dropping down before the bungee cord runs out

D = 2

Pitch:
rock climbing – a distance all the group climbs before you move on to the next stage

There are strange names for tricks too. In extreme kayaking a "wave wheel" is a trick where you use a wave to get your kayak upright in the water and then slam it down again.

Rope

You can't water-ski without rope.

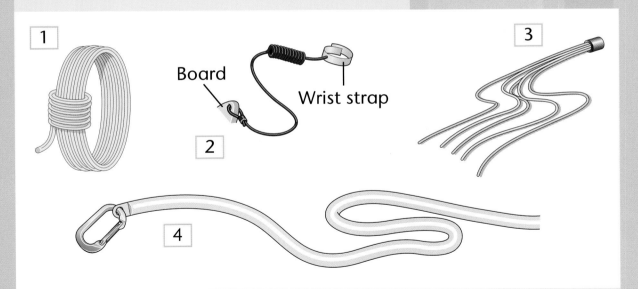

1

Board

Wrist strap

3

2

4

Can you name four other extreme sports that need these ropes?

For help, look through the book.

Many extreme sports need some kind of rope.

1 Rock climbing

2 Boogie boarding

3 Paragliding

4 Bungee jumping

Can you think of any other extreme sports that use rope?